The Very Hungry Mosquito

Jack Gabolinscy
Connah Brecon

NELSON
CENGAGE Learning™

Australia • Brazil • Japan • Korea • Mexico • Singapore • Spain • United Kingdom • United States

NELSON
CENGAGE Learning™

The Very Hungry Mosquito

Text: Jack Gabolinscy
Illustrations: Connah Brecon
Editor: Rebecca Crisp
Design: James Lowe
Series design: James Lowe
Production controller: Lisa Porter
Reprint: Siew Han Ong

Fast Forward Independent Texts
Level 6

ISBN 978 0 17 017915 7
ISBN 978 0 17 017896 9 (set)

Cengage Learning Australia
Level 7, 80 Dorcas Street
South Melbourne, Victoria Australia 3205
Phone: 1300 790 853

Cengage Learning New Zealand
Unit 4B Rosedale Office Park
331 Rosedale Road, Albany, North Shore NZ 0632
Phone: 0508 635 766

For learning solutions, visit **cengage.com.au**

Printed in Australia by Ligare Pty Ltd
3 4 5 6 7 22 21 20

The Very Hungry Mosquito

Jack Gabolinscy
Connah Brecon

Contents

Chapter 1	**Dinner Time**	**4**
Chapter 2	**You Can't Suck My Blood**	**6**
Chapter 3	**A Big Balloon**	**14**

Dinner Time

At dinner time,
a very hungry mosquito flew over the trees.
He looked down
and saw all of the animals.

"Good," he said.
"There is lots of blood for my dinner."

The animals looked up
and saw the very hungry mosquito.

"Oh no!" they said.
"Not him again."

CHAPTER 2

You Can't Suck My Blood

The very hungry mosquito
saw an elephant
drinking some water.
He flew down
to suck its blood.

"Go away," shouted the elephant.
"You can't suck my blood."

The very hungry mosquito saw a tiger and flew down to suck its blood.

"No! No! Go away!" shouted the tiger.
"You can't suck my blood."

The very hungry mosquito saw a monkey sleeping in a tree.
He flew down to suck its blood.

"Oh no," shouted the monkey.
"You can't suck my blood."

The very hungry mosquito
saw a dog and a cat.
He flew down to suck their blood.

"No! No! You can't suck my blood," shouted the dog.

"No! No! You can't suck my blood," shouted the cat.

CHAPTER 3

A Big Balloon

The very hungry mosquito saw a girl sleeping under a tree.

He flew down to suck her blood.

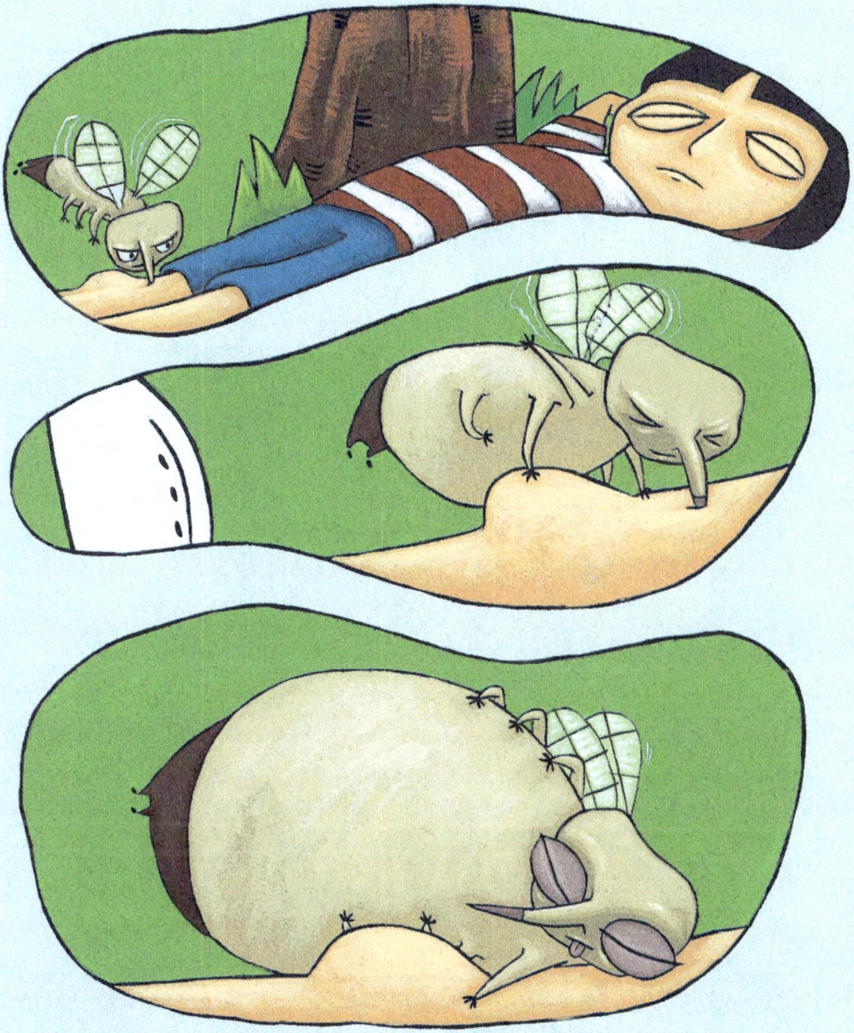

He sucked and sucked.
He sucked
until he was as big as a balloon.

Then he fell asleep.

When the girl woke up
she saw the fat mosquito
sleeping on her leg.
She was not happy.

Smack!
She squashed the fat mosquito.

"You can't suck my blood now," she said.